The Hiram Reunion.

POEM AND ADDRESS,

TOGETHER WITH THE

CONSTITUTION AND OFFICERS

OF THE SOCIETY.

JUNE 14, 1867.

CLEVELAND, OHIO:

1867.

History.

The first Reunion of ECLECTIC Students was held at Hiram, August 31st, 1866. The call was informal and the notice short, yet there was a large assemblage of students and friends. After spending the day and evening together, it was resolved to continue the reunions. A Managing Committee, consisting of two ladies and three gentlemen, was appointed. This Committee made choice of Friday after Commencement, June 14th, 1867, as the day for the second reunion. The Committee also made arrangements for a Poem and an Address. The reunion took place on the day mentioned—a joyous meeting of old and new friends. It was decided to form a Society. This decision was carried into effect by adopting a Constitution, and electing Officers. Arrangements were also made for publishing the proceedings of the day. This little publication is sent out in the hope that it will be kindly received by those to whom it is especially commended—the old and new students of the ECLECTIC.

POEM.

BY ALMEDA A. BOOTH.

We come to meet them here,
Our friends from far and near;
To meet with love sincere and true,
Eclectic friends both old and new,
And welcome give.

Away with toil and care,
'Mid scenes so bright and fair;
The bustling world bid go its way,
And let, for one unfettered day,
The past re-live.

The playful mind at ease,
Its sportive self will please
With ringing laugh and merry jest,
And find no harmless mirth repressed,
Or awed by fears.

Here kindling eyes will greet,
When friend with friend shall meet;
Here hearts will ache and tears will flow,
When recollection back shall go
To other years.

On this familiar ground
Inspiring life we found,
While toilsome years, yet peaceful days,
Went hast'ning on their changeful ways,
With ceaseless flow.

Here eyes were calm and bright,
And hearts were pure and light;
Here notes of joyous hope were sung,
And brows were fair and souls were young
With gen'rous glow.

Here kindred hearts were found,
And friends for life were bound;
Here Love threw round his mystic chain,
One link of joy and one of pain,
In sweet accord.

Here truth and love divine
Did heart and soul refine,
When peace and trusting faith began
A pure and noble life for man,
By grace restored.

Here high resolve grew strong,
To battle 'gainst the wrong;
Ambition sat with folded wing,
Not dreaming yet that fame would bring
Exalted place.

Here nature, too, we love—
The earth, the skies above;
We love full well the distant view,

Where landscape meets the ether blue
In fond embrace.

At early hour of dawn,
O'er hill and sloping lawn,
How beautiful the rising mist,
When morning beam its face has kissed
With rosy blush;

A broad and shallow lake,
Where tree-tops islands make;
Then morn bequeaths her mist to noon
For mantle blue, but reddened soon
In evening flush.

A lovely home for truth
To guide the steps of youth,
Where peace and innocence control,
And quiet beauty leads the soul
In wisdom's ways.

In weary hours and sad,
When life is darkly clad,
In hours when passions fiercely burn,
Regretful mem'ry here will turn
To tranquil days.

Our alma-mater true
Has numbered years but few;
These children lads and lasses grown,
Ere yet was laid her corner-stone;
She is not old.

Amid her youthful scenes,
In truth she's in her teens,
Yet stories long she could relate,
Adventures strange and changes great
By her be told.

She saw the grandest sight,
A nation's rising might;
She saw, when deadly conflict rose,
Her children fall by southern foes
A sacrifice.

She gave with prayers and tears,
With mingled hopes and fears,
Her bravest sons, her treasures rare;
In silent grief she leaves them there,
Where glory lies.

She saw fell slavery gone,
And hailed a brighter dawn;
Redeemed, she felt the nation stand,
And looked upon her native land
As saved anew.

No party name she wears—
No factious spirit shares;
For human kind she sets no bar;
The sons of earth all brothers are,
Though strange their hue.

As washed on either side
Her country is by ocean tide,
She looks for millions yet to go

O'er sunny plains and hills of snow,
In mingled throng.

She sees a ripening field,
That harvests rich will yield
Of human souls, but reapers few,
And trusts her sons she may imbue
With purpose strong.

She boasts no high-born name—
Plebeian is her fame;
No lordly footstep in her halls,
No courtly grace within her walls,
No pride of birth.

Yet elegance refined
She seeks and hopes to find
In daughters gentle, sons well-bred;
For noble rank, she takes instead
Their modest worth.

New names for mater dear,
As college, we shall hear;
Though titles such she choose to don,
No airs we think she's putting on,
She has good sense.

With titles old or new,
We know she's staunch and true;
If graceful honors she may wear,
For names her children little care
Nor take offense.

She sits like nature's queen,
To rule this goodly scene;
While mind with thought she fills,
As pure as snow that drifts her hills
In winter time.

Observed on every side,
Her light she may not hide,
For nature's laws she's called to bound
With rev'rent care, and show what's found
In every clime.

Between the scoffer's rant
And bigot's idle cant
The line of truth is her's to scan,
To show "the ways of God to man,"
And faith restore.

Still for some good she'll seek
In Latin and in Greek.
These noble tongues she'll not desert,
Till reason strong shall her convert
From classic lore.

On her may fortune smile,
Her name no blot defile;
May long and vig'rous life be hers,
The fame that honest worth confers
Her rightful meed.

May heaven's holy page,
For all, in youth and age,
Its richest, highest blessings bring,
O'er all a crown, a glory fling,
Our greatest need.

ADDRESS.

BY B. A. HINSDALE.

OLD AND NEW FRIENDS:

You have not assembled on this interesting occasion for the purpose of listening to a long and labored address. The most beautiful thoughts, dropped from the most eloquent lips, could not, and should not, make you forget the object of our meeting. It is to revive the old time, to live over the old life, to strengthen friendships decaying through lapse of time, that we have come together. We have come to look into the windows through which the light of our study-lamps once shone, to walk through the rooms where once we recited, to tread the ground where once we trod, some of us with lighter step and freer heart than now, to annihilate the time that has sped away since we left these pleasant scenes, to think of the absent living and of the absent dead.

We boys have come to mingle again in the fray of debate, to recount the triumphs of the past, to ask the girls with whom we walked and talked when younger than now, to sit with us under the shade of the trees, around whose roots we carefully sifted the mellow earth in the spring-time long gone by. And you girls have come to revive in memory the generous emulations of other days, and to talk, in your modest way, with the boys at whose knock you were once accustomed to throw open your doors on Saturday afternoons. These are the objects of our assembling, and not to listen to a formal address. You do not expect me to unfold any theme philosophic, historic, political, or literary; nor is such my purpose. Neither is it in my head or heart to detain you long.

However it might be at other re-unions, there is but one line of thought proper to be presented at this, and that is suggested by the circumstances under which we have come together. The future is *not* to be as the past; old things are to pass away, all things are to become new. Some words and phrases that we have loved are to fall into disuse; other words and phrases, strange, and to some of us uncouth, are to supersede them. ECLECTIC INSTITUTE—name never to be forgotten!—gives place to Hiram College; "new students" and "advanced students," yield their places to Freshmen and Seniors; the unpretending "teachers," who taught us in the good old time, resign their chairs to Professors; and, *miserabile visu et dictu*, "old students" will be followed by a full-fledged brood of Alumni; and then such words as "graduate" and "under-graduate," "diploma" and "degree," will figure in the new terminology to the shame and confusion of those of us who are doomed to get on through life, as best we may, without sheepskin backing. This re-union sees the last of the *old* school, sad as the thought may be. Soon we may say:

"His face is growing sharp and thin,
Alack! our friend is gone.
Close up his eyes; tie up his chin;
Step from the corpse and let him in
That standeth there alone,
And waiteth at the door.
There is a new foot on the floor, my friend,
And a new face at the door, my friend,
A new face at the door."

And yet before we "let him in," let us fix

clearly in our minds the form and features of the friend whose place he takes. Of course I shall be obliged to talk a good deal about ourselves, but that, under the circumstances, will be allowable. There are some occasions when egotism is not only pardoned but expected, and I presume school re-unions may be reckoned among them. Somewhere I have read of a German whose self respect was so great that he never referred to himself without taking off his hat. In imitation of this complacent German, let us don our hats and proceed to draw out a historic sketch that will be in part a record of our own achievements and virtues.

Like most great characters, the Eclectic Institute was born of poor but respectable parents. Its coming was without observation. Its life has been one of toil and trial. It has lived on through seventeen years solely because it won its way to the hearts of the people. And still the truth compels me to say that since these grounds were purchased, this building erected, and both paid for, the teachers who have taught in these halls have made the only considerable sacrifices that have been made in its behalf. I will take the responsibility of saying that in these seventeen years, no school in the State, having at its command no greater resources, has done more for the cause of education. Eclectic students are still young men and young women. And the next ten or twenty years will emphasize the statement that they have won for themselves high places of usefulness and honor in society. Eclectic boys have wrought nobly; in the school-room, on the farm; in the army, on the editorial staff; in the pulpit, at the bar. As a class they do not fail but succeed. And then Eclectic girls are a very *manly* sort of girls; they make good wives and mothers, and no higher compliment could be paid them even in the age of Rosa Bonheur, Elizabeth Barrett, and Anna Dickenson.

Standing then as we do to-day on the pivotal point in the Eclectic's history, it is well worth our while to inquire, What have been the ruling ideas that have insured this success in the past and that deserve to be perpetuated in the future? Of these ideas there are three, and I shall name them, but without any attempt to put them in the order of their value or prominence.

First, I shall name the idea of a self-reliant manhood—that interior force or energy which enables its possessor to stand up on his own individuality, and work his way to success.—Many institutions are surrounded by an effeminating, emasculating atmosphere, that unfits the man who breathes it for the real work of life. If you immerse a bone in some acids the earthy matter is removed, and only a soft, plastic, gelatinous pulp is left; so these institutions destroy the very skeleton of character and leave a spongy moluscous creature, entirely unable to push his way in the world. Such institutions may give expansion to the mind and gentleness to the heart, but they are not the sort of institutions for to-day. They could be tolerated in the past when the difference between the scholar and the worker was more clearly defined than now, when learning was a guild and protected by the conventionalities of society; but now when the scholar is *beginning* to be a worker, and the worker is *beginning* to be a scholar, they will not supply our educational wants. Buckle, in one of his essays, inveighs strenuously, almost bitterly, against the weakness and helplessness of literary men; but the fact which he deplores is due, in large measure, to the failure of schools, colleges, and universities to infuse into their students a self-reliant manhood. The scholar who is unable to take care of himself, who is a pauper upon the world, deservedly falls into contempt. Young men have here been taught that success is *in the man*, and does not grow out of fortuitous circumstances; they have been taught to preach their own sermons, make their own speeches, teach their own schools, and that theirs will be the success and theirs the failure.

One important part of this healthy discipline has been to impress the desirability, the necessity even, of being able to do more than one thing. Division of labor, as the economists call it, is good, essential indeed to the progress of society, but there is some reason to fear that it is being pushed too far. It is well to have more than one string to your bow, whether you spell it b-o-w or b-e-a-u. The results of this kind of discipline are very observable. Eclectic students are able to take care of themselves.—Other schools may send forth more finished scholars, but none send out more helpful men and women. I know no Eclectic students who are learned paupers—none who are begging their bread and cheese.

As the second of these ideas, I shall name that

of a muscular morality reinforced by a practical religion. The motto has been, "Quit you like men, be strong." Too often has morality been divorced from manliness, and religion from character; the one being made to consist of dry ethical formulas without heart, and the other of pietistic mouthings without life. One of the most painful chapters in the history of the Church, is that in which we read of religion being driven away into the wilderness of dogma and formula, to be tempted and overcome by the devil; and in the future one of the most pleasing chapters will be that in which men read of its return to the abodes of man, to be reanimated by the Spirit of God.

It has often been set down to the credit of the Eclectic that from her walls have gone forth a large number of preachers, and justly so. But the number of theologians, in the technical sense of the term, has been small. I shall not be sorry if that number is not materially increased in the future. It is expected that more attention will hereafter be paid to fitting men for the ministry. I bid those who have this work at heart a god-speed; and yet with all my love for these walls, fragrant with the memories of the past, I would rather see them crumble back to the clay and limestone of which they were made, than to hear them echo the footfalls of mouthers of formulas, peddlers of dogmas, and hunters of heresy.

This institution has done something, as I verily believe, in calling the attention of men back to more wholesome ideas concerning religion. I fervently hope that the idea here unfolded, a muscular morality reinforced by practical religion, under whose benign influence so many noble natures have expanded in the past, will be the pole-star of the future.

As the third and last of these ideas, I name the free spirit, the intellectual toleration, the large-mindedness that has characterized the Eclectic. Nothing destroys a man sooner or more effectually than narrowness. What the mind needs is room. We want roomy men, roomy books, roomy schools. Men are surrounded by an atmosphere. You have breathed the close, oppressive, stifling atmosphere, laden with the carbonic acid gas of party and sect, that envelopes some men. From such an atmosphere you feel that you must escape or die of mental asphyxia. Again you have met men of a broad horizon of thought, their intellectual boundaries stretching away on every side beyond your fartherest reach. The atmosphere of these is bracing, invigorating, full of the oxygen of our modern civilization. You will cry out in exultation, "Here I can grow to the extent of my capabilities."

What I have said of men holds true of books. Some are small, narrow, seven by nine, where you will die of suffocation; others are large, roomy, where you are in no danger of being cramped to death. It holds true also of schools. From some a large, roomy-minded man never goes forth. For an extreme case take the schools of the Jesuits. For two centuries in them was trained the best mind of the Catholic church; who can name a mind of the first order, or even of the second, that they gave to the world? Other schools have the power of enlarging what is small, of expanding what is narrow, of making liberal, if not great, thinkers out of average minds. It therefore becomes all who have their own healthy growth at heart, to be sure of the atmosphere before they take a man, a book, or a school into their confidence.

For a school to be roomy it is not necessary

for it to be either old or rich; not necessary that it have numerous and costly buildings or colossal libraries. Indeed these, insuring as they frequently do conservatism, may defeat the very end in view. Look at Oxford. Its name carries us back to the time of the Saxons.—There, says Goldwin Smith, "are the annals of England written in gray stone." It was a place of education in the time of Alfred, whose birthplace was hard by. It was afterwards the home of Duns Scotus, of Occam, of Wickliffe. According to one of the old chroniclers, in the reign of Henry III, 30,000 students gathered there to attend the lectures. There are the venerable colleges founded by Walter de Merton, William of Durham, and Cardinal Wolsey. There is the great Bodleian library, rich in the tomes of all languages and all ages. All this excites our interest and fires our imagination, and yet the writer just mentioned says, "Nowhere do you feel more the power of the past, and the ascendency of the dead over the living. This influence, in truth, weighs somewhat too heavily on the intellectual life of Oxford. An Oxford student can preserve his independence and even his individual activity of mind, only by cultivating a very large and liberal interest in the general fortunes and destinies of humanity." True, indeed! When has Oxford championed a single cause whose purpose was to give more room to Man? It is no wonder that the iconoclastic Puritans dealt so harshly, savagely even, with this famous seat of learning. But, thank God, we can have room without asking leave of venerable universities. Says a recent writer: "The great revolutionists have generally been cradled in mangers, and have gone through rough discipline in early life. Civilization is indebted to lowly cradles, and unknown mothers hold a heavy account against the world."

I am crying out against narrowness. God cries out against it too. In Nature, in Revelation, in History, He enters His protests. Let us take one or two illustrations from the latter. With all my veneration for the Scriptures, highly as I value our Christian civilization, essential even to the temporal welfare of man as I conceive the Gospel to be, I am still compelled to say that Christendom is too assuming. Every fair-minded man must concede that there are sources of culture, intellectual, æsthetic, moral even, for which we are indebted neither to Christianity nor to the Church. There is a significance of which some of us may not be aware, in the fact that the Greeks, believers as they were in Zeus, and Pan, and Apollo, held the gateway of the West in the face of Eastern invasion until the political independence of Europe was secured, laid the foundations of science, sounded the depths of philosophy, cultivated all forms of æsthetic expression, in a word, kindled the torch of knowledge that the after generations are proud to hand on, blown into a fiercer flame, to the coming ages.

Again, Christendom has never acknowledged its obligations to Islam. The stream of Christian civilization has received few broader affluents than that which sprung from the little oasis in Arabia, where stood the city of Medina. It entered Europe from the West. It gathered a mighty head in the schools of Toledo and Cordova, only to flow over the Pyrenees into France and Sicily. It watered the south of France, the beautiful provinces of Provence and Languedoc, and there blossomed out the freest life that Europe had known for centuries. Freedom of thought gave birth to heresy, as the church termed it, and heresy to persecution. While

Europe was indebted to the Mohammedans, together with the Jews, for this free development, it was the bishop who claimed to sit in Peter's chair, and who certainly ruled all that was left in Europe of the churches founded by the labors of Peter and Paul, who inaugurated the crusade which devastated those Provinces, destroyed learning, hushed the song of the Troubadour, and made the green hillsides and valleys run red with blood.

These are large facts and well worth our study. They are God's protests in History against the narrowness of men. They prove that each nation has its work to do, that "men of every clime and race are necessary to make up the entire of God's idea of humanity." Still we must not forget that these streams are only affluents feeding the stream of Christian civilization which is sweeping on to the ocean of the world's destiny. The Ohio feeds the Mississippi; the Mississippi flows to the sea! The Pagan civilization of Greece is dead, and so is the Mohammedan civilization of Arabia and Spain; but the waters of these two affluents make up no small share of the larger stream upon which we ride.

This is what I mean when I say the spirit of the Eclectic has been free, tolerant, large-minded. Here we have had room. As a class Eclectic students are neither partisans in the State nor sectaries in the Church. The three ideas which I have unfolded, have been the dominant ones in the Eclectic polity. I do not say that no others should be incorporated with them in the future; but this I say, I shall be sorry to see any of these abandoned.

I have referred to the change that is to occur in the character of the school. The Board of Trustees has decided that the Eclectic Institute shall be Hiram College. This is not the place to discuss the wisdom of its action. Indeed, such discussion will be of little profit at any time. The decree has gone forth; the child is born. If those who stood sponsors for it at the baptism are perplexed to find swaddling bands to cover its nakedness, it does not concern us. What I call upon every one sharing in this reunion to do, what I call upon every Hiram student to do, is to stand by the College. It will be a new friend, but it will have an old face; we will cherish the daughter because we have loved the mother. I do not mean that we are to be its fulsome eulogists, its narrow partisans. That cannot be asked at our hands. To be such we must forget the liberal teaching of the past, and that I, for one, can never do. But what I mean is this: that the weight of our influence—and we are numerous enough and old enough to have some influence—shall be on its side.

The character and fate of a school are largely in the hands of those who have enjoyed its benefits.

The Alumni of a College, when they become numerous, can make or unmake it; and the thousands who have been taught in these halls can be of very essential service to this institution in this the crisis of its history. I have said the crisis of its history. Such it is. Two or three years, and perhaps much less time, will determine whether it is to be *more* or *less* than it has been; perhaps they will determine whether it is to be *more* or *nothing*. Let us not then go from this reunion to our homes, until we have pledged ourselves to the new enterprise.

Old school friends: I am glad to be able to meet you at this reunion. It does me good to look into your faces and to hear your words. We need sympathy and intercommunication of thought. As we give ourselves to our "heavy job of work," we frequently stagger and almost fall under the burthen. Sometimes my heart sinks, and I say, I might as well try and push over one of the pyramids by laying my hand against it, as to try to raise men to a higher plane of life. You, I doubt not, have similar feelings. We will go to our homes and to our work, stronger for having shared together the joys of this anniversary.

Many whom we would have been pleased to see and take by the hand, are not with us. Some whose hearts are here are detained at home by their business; some, like the members of an ancient church, have lost their first love and are kept away by their indifference; some, though I trust the number is not large, may have fallen into evil ways and have not cared to show their faces; some rest in known and some in unknown graves. While we remember all these in kindness, dropping a tear for the dead and putting up a prayer for the fallen, let us thank the Infinite Father that so many have been able to meet together.

Still farther: let us not abandon these re-unions. They will do us and the college good. We shall value them more and more highly as older we grow. Pretty soon an occasional "old fellow" will get "mixed with the boys;" and as we go sweeping past mile-stone after mile-stone along the high-road of life, as one after another falls out of the column and is borne away by strong arms to a home on the hillock or in the valley, there to rest under the shade of green trees until the Father calls him; as we increase in wisdom and in goodness, those who keep their hearts young will more and more love to come up to these annual rallyings.

Nor must I close without a word for the future. Great things have come to pass since the feet of some of us first pressed these floors. We behold a country freed from the giant sin of its youth. A new era is opening. There is work to be done for the country, for man, for God. Upon the American scholar devolves no light responsibility. Shall we not return from this anniversary to our homes resolved to do our share?

"We are living, we are dwelling
In a grand and awful time,

In an age on ages telling;
  To be living is sublime.

Hark! the onset! will ye fold your
  Faith-clad arms in lazy lock?
Up! O, up! thou drowsy soldier;
  Worlds are charging to the shock.

Worlds are charging, heaven beholding;
  Thou hast but an hour to fight;
Now, the blazoned crown unfolding,
  On! right onward for the right.

On! let all the soul within you
  For the truth's sake go abroad;
Strike! let every nerve and sinew
  Tell on ages—tell for God."

CONSTITUTION.

We, the former and present Students of the Eclectic Institute, at this Reunion assembled, do hereby organize ourselves into a society based on the following Constitution:

For the purpose of perpetuating the pleasant memories of our student life at Hiram, we hereby ordain and establish a society to be known as The Hiram Reunion.

Article 1. The officers of this Society shall consist of a Master of Ceremonies, Alternate, and Scribe, to be elected annually.

Article 2. In addition to their usual duties, these officers shall constitute an Executive Committee to make all arrangements for the annual meeting of the society, which shall be held Commencement week.

Article 3. The following persons are hereby declared life members of this society:

1st. All who at any time are or have been Students, Teachers, Lecturers or Trustees of the Institution at Hiram.

2d. All husbands and wives of such Students, Teachers, Lecturers or Trustees.

OFFICERS.

J. A. Garfield, - *Master of Ceremonies.*

H. M. James, - - - - - - - *Alternate.*

Mrs. Hettie Smith Clark, - - *Scribe.*